Seven Years and a day

Colette O'Hare & Beryl Cook

Collins

For The Belle of Bootle

First published in Great Britain 1980
by William Collins Sons & Co Ltd

ISBN 0 00 195745 7

Colour origination Acolortone Ltd
Made and printed in Great Britain by
William Collins Sons and Co Ltd Glasgow

"We're going to have to get another cat," said Mr. Mulholland. "Them mice is getting as bold as brass." He and Mrs. Mulholland had just returned from their weekly visit to the club. He was just hanging up his overcoat and muffler on the hallstand when he saw a mouse scoot underneath.

"Cats," snorted Mrs. Mulholland, who hadn't noticed it, "just eat you out of house and home."

But Mr. Mulholland smiled a little smile to himself. There was nothing nicer than having a cat about the place.

The next morning, though, Mrs. Mulholland found a mouse in the bread bin. That was enough to convince even her. She put on her coat and she was away round to her sister's place. It was always teeming with cats.

Big Madge, Mrs. Mulholland's sister, had her hands full as usual. "I think there's one in the coalhole," she shouted above the noise of the telly and young Liam, "or maybe under the chair."

Mrs. Mulholland was soon back home.

"I got one," she said, as she emptied a pillowcase out onto the mat, "and look at that will you, it's got six toes on both of its front paws. She'd never have parted with it if she'd noticed that."

For it was said that if you were kind to a six-toed cat and treated it well for seven years and a day, it would grant your dearest wish.

Well, from then on in, Mrs. Mulholland's attitude to cats changed entirely.

It was the cat this, and the cat that. There wasn't a cat in the county who got better treatment.

"Don't sit there," Mrs. Mulholland told her husband, "that's the cat's chair."

Poor Mr. Mulholland was relegated to a draughty corner by the door, usually reserved for Big Madge when she came round for the loan of something.

"Only one sausage?" asked Mr. Mulholland timidly as his tea was put on the table that night.

"Correct," said Mrs. Mulholland, fixing him with a terrible stare, "only one sausage. That cat's got to be looked after."

After that Mr. Mulholland ate his meals, such as they were, in the scullery.

Quite often when Mrs. Mulholland was out at the shops, and the cat sat staring calmly at him with its great green eyes, Mr. Mulholland would say:

"Well now . . . aren't you the fine one . . . leading us all a dance . . . but . . . what's the use of complaining to you . . . you're only a dumb animal."

The cat made no sign, just drew its twelve front claws rhythmically in and out of Mr. Mulholland's well upholstered knees.

As the nights grew longer and the wind turned really bitter Mr. Mulholland just thought he'd enquire where his hot water bottle was, but he knew it was a silly question.

The years wore on. As the seventh year and a day of the cat's stay with the Mulhollands approached, Mrs. Mulholland became more and more anxious and attentive. The cat wanted for nothing. Mr. and Mrs. Mulholland slept in the spare room with its peeling wallpaper and itchy, threadbare blankets.

The cat, meanwhile, snuggled down in the big bed with its comfortable bolster pillows and fluffy flannelette sheets and the plump, faded pink satin eiderdown which had been a wedding present from Mr. Mulholland's Aunt Esther. And as the mill sirens went and the watery grey morning light filtered through the good curtains, the cat yawned and stretched and went back to sleep.

If it lay in Mr. Mulholland's marrow patch, he was not permitted to shoo it away.

"By Jingo," said Mr. Mulholland, "if ever a man suffered. . . ."

The cat got the top of the milk, with a drop of whisky added of a Saturday.

On Sunday it enjoyed a plate of roast for its dinner and cooked ham for its tea.

"You must be feeding that man of yours well," said Francie in the fish shop when Mrs. Mulholland came in twice in one week.

"Never you mind what I'm doing," Mrs. Mulholland told him coldly.

But Francie wasn't the only one to notice how extravagant Mrs. Mulholland had become with the housekeeping.

"You're fairly getting through the milk these days, Mrs. Mulholland," said Brendan the milkman, "what are you doing? Having a bath in it?"

Mrs Mulholland
12 pints

Despite Mrs. Mulholland's efforts to keep it a secret, word had of course got out about the cat's magical powers. The entire neighbourhood followed the progress of the whole to-do with great interest.

Wherever Mrs. Mulholland went, she was watched by speculative eyes, and followed by hordes of children, while dozens more pressed their noses to the parlour window, or swung on the garden gate hoping to catch a sight of the six-toed cat.

Mr. Mulholland had to admit that he'd be glad when it was all over. And at long last he was able to announce to his wife: "Mary Agnes – today's the day!"

"What is?" She was putting more coal on the fire in case the cat began to feel the cold.

"Today," said Mr. Mulholland, "she's been with us seven years and a day."

"Oh, devil the bit of it," said Mrs. Mulholland crossly, for she hated being called Mary Agnes, "it's *tomorrow*. And what's it to you anyway?

I'm the one who's been taking good care of her."

"I'm telling you," Mr. Mulholland insisted, "it's today."

Mrs. Mulholland raked the fire with a vigour that made the coal spit.

"Oooh," she sighed with exasperation, "the older you get, the harder you are to live with. I wish I was a thousand miles away from here!"

And suddenly she was.

Mr. Mulholland gazed with amazement as the poker clattered to the hearth.

It was strange really. You'd have expected a puff of blue smoke. Or even a little streak of lightning. But no, there was nothing like that. It was just that Mrs. Mulholland wasn't there any more.

The cat drew its six-toed claws rhythmically in and out of the cushion on Mr. Mulholland's chair, and he thought he detected a sly glint in those great green eyes.

"So now," said Mr. Mulholland, "and what would you like for your tea?"

The pictures are for Alexa